3/08

Kelly Clarkson

Kelly Clarkson

by Laurie Collier Hillstrom

LUCENT BOOKS

An imprint of Thomson Gale, a part of The Thomson Corporation

THOMSON

™

GALE

Detroit • New York • San Francisco • New Haven, Conn. • Waterville, Maine • London

For more information, contact:
Lucent Books
27500 Drake Rd.
Farmington Hills, MI 48331-3535
Or you can visit our Internet site at http://www.gale.com

LIBRARY OF CONGRESS CATALOGING-IN-PUBLICATION DATA

Hillstrom, Laurie Collier, 1965–
    Kelly Clarkson / by Laurie Collier Hillstrom.
        p. cm. — (People in the news)
    Includes bibliographical references (p.   ) and index.
    ISBN: 978-1-4205-0013-4 (hardcover)
    1. Clarkson, Kelly—Juvenile literature. 2. Singers—United States—Biography—Juvenile literature. I. Title.
    ML3930.C523H55 2008
    782.42164092—dc22
    [B]
                                                                        2007035911

ISBN-10: 1-4205-0013-9

Contents

Fame and celebrity are fascinating. We are drawn toward people who walk in fame's spotlight, whether they are known for great achievements or for famous acts. The lives of celebrities attract attention, perhaps because their experiences seem in some ways so different from, yet in other ways so similar to, our own.

Newspapers, magazines, and television regularly take advantage of our fascination by running profiles of famous people. For example, television programs such as *Entertainment Tonight* devote all their programming to stories about entertainment and entertainers. Magazines such as *People* fill their pages with stories of the private lives of famous people. Even newspapers, newsmagazines, and television news frequently look at the lives of well-known personalities. But despite the number of articles and programs on offer, few provide us with more than a superficial glimpse of celebrity life.

Lucent's People in the News series offers young readers a closer look at the lives of today's newsmakers, the influences that have shaped them, and the impact they have had on the world, and on other people's lives. The subjects of the series come from many disciplines and walks of life. They include authors, musicians, athletes, political leaders, entertainers, entrepreneurs, and others who have made a mark on modern life and who, in many cases, will continue to do so for years to come.

These biographies are more than just factual accounts. Each book emphasizes the contributions, achievements, or deeds that have brought fame to the individual. The books also show how that person has influenced modern life. Authors describe their subjects in a realistic, unsentimental light. For example, Bill Gates—the cofounder and chief executive officer of the software giant Microsoft—has made personal computers the most vital tool of the modern age. Few dispute his business skills, his perseverance, or his technical expertise, but critics say he is ruthless in his dealings with competitors and is driven more by his desire to maintain Microsoft's dominance in the computer industry than by an interest in furthering technology.

In these books, young readers will encounter inspiring stories about real people who have achieved success despite enormous obstacles. Oprah Winfrey—the most powerful, most watched, and wealthiest woman on television today—spent the first six years of her life in the care of her grandparents while her unwed mother sought work and a better life elsewhere. Her adolescence was colored by promiscuity, pregnancy at age fourteen, rape, and sexual abuse.

Each author documents and supports his or her work with a selection of primary and secondary source quotations taken from diaries, letters, speeches, and interviews. All quotes are footnoted to show readers exactly how and where biographers got their information, and provide guidance for further research. The quotations bring the text to life by giving readers eyewitness accounts of the life and achievements of each person covered in the People in the News series.

In addition, each book in the series includes photographs, annotated bibliographies, timelines, and comprehensive indexes. For both the casual reader and the student researcher, the People in the News series offers an insight into the lives of today's newsmakers—people who shape the way we live, work, and play in the modern age.

Charting Her Own Course

For many people, Kelly Clarkson will always be known as the first winner of the reality-TV singing competition *American Idol*. In 2002, during the first season of this extremely popular talent show, Clarkson captured the hearts of millions of television viewers with her powerful voice and appealing stage presence. Week after week, as her competitors failed to make it through the competition, Clarkson gave strong performances that earned praise from the judges. On the final episode, with over 22 million television viewers tuned in, she gained the grand prize of a million-dollar recording contract.

Because Clarkson's big break into the music business had such a dramatic, fairytale quality to it, many people think that her road to stardom has always been easy. In reality, however, Clarkson has been through some rough times. Her parents divorced when she was young, for example, and she had several frustrating attempts trying to launch a career as a singer. Few *American Idol* viewers were aware of Clarkson's background when they enjoyed her confident performances and her outgoing personality on the show.

After she won *American Idol*, Clarkson's connection with the show meant that many critics questioned her natural ability. They thought she had achieved stardom purely through luck and effective marketing. During a whirlwind of interviews, promotional appearances, recording sessions, concert tours, and film shoots, Clarkson continually struggled to prove herself worthy of all the attention she received.

Kelly Clarkson's powerful voice and stage presence helped her win the first season of **American Idol.**

Kelly Clarkson's artistic ambition has helped propel her career and earn respect throughout the music industry.

Clarkson has also faced an ongoing battle to be taken seriously within the recording industry. Since she began work on her first album in 2002, Clarkson has shown a great deal of artistic ambition—she has always pressured recording executives to allow her to write her own songs and to take control over the direction of her career. But even after her second album sold 6 million copies and won two Grammy Awards, Clarkson's desire to express herself and grow as an artist was still met with opposition from her record label. This led to a well-documented controversy over the content of her third album in 2007.

Despite the challenges Clarkson has faced as the first winner of *American Idol*, she has often shown how grateful she is for the exposure and opportunities that the show has given her. "People have the wrong idea, like I don't want to talk about it," she said. "I think it's a great thing. It was obviously the best way for me to come into the business and it's just a great opportunity for everyday normal people. It's like a Cinderella story every day."[1]

On the other hand, Clarkson realizes that her association with the show has often made it difficult for her to be taken seriously as an artist. In order to gain respect for her talents as a singer and songwriter, Clarkson eventually had to distance herself from *American Idol*. Instead of trying to hold on to the instant fame she gained from the show, Clarkson worked hard to build a lasting music career. "Fame is exactly what I thought it would be. It's hard and a lot of sacrifices," she explained. "If I could do without the fame part of it, I think I would. Basically I'm here for the fans and here for my music."[2]

In the years that followed her appearance on *American Idol*, Clarkson has earned the respect of many fans, critics, and people in the recording industry for her determination to stand up for herself and to chart the course of her own career. "Back in the day, female artists were told to perform and then go sit in the corner," said country music legend Reba McEntire. "Thank God for people like [country music legend and successful busi-nesswoman] Dolly Parton who took charge. Kelly is the same way. She knows what she wants. She's had a rough go of it in the music business. People think she just won *Idol* and every-thing else was easy. Not so. She's had to fight."[3] Clarkson's drive, ambition, and independent spirit have helped her to move beyond her fame as a reality-show winner and achieve success on her own terms.

Chapter 1

A Small-Town Texas Girl

Before Kelly Clarkson rocketed to pop music stardom on *American Idol*, she developed a strong sense of self and an independent spirit while growing up in a small Texas town. These qualities helped her get through some rough times, including her parents' divorce and her early struggles to launch a career as a singer.

An Unsettled Early Childhood

Kelly Brianne Clarkson was born on April 24, 1982, in Fort Worth, Texas. Her mother, Jeanne Ann Rose, was an elementary school teacher, while her father, Stephen Michael Clarkson, worked as an engineer and car salesman. When Kelly was six years old, her parents divorced after seventeen years of marriage. The divorce divided Kelly's family and forced her to become more self-reliant.

After the divorce, Kelly's older brother, Jason, stayed with their father, who moved to Anaheim, California. Her older sister, Alyssa, went to live with an aunt. Only Kelly remained with their mother. Over the next few years, Kelly and her mother moved several times within Texas. Kelly missed her father and her brother and sister, and she found it difficult to adjust to new schools and different neighborhoods. In addition, as she told one interviewer, "there were always worries financially"[4] during this difficult time.

After her parents' divorce, Kelly's older brother Jason, pictured, moved away with their father while Kelly stayed with her mother.

Kelly's life became more stable and secure when her mother remarried and the new family settled in Burleson, Texas, about ten miles south of Fort Worth. Kelly's family grew to include a stepfather, building contractor Jimmy Taylor, and five older step-siblings at this time.

Born to Perform

Despite the difficulties she faced as a child, Kelly was a friendly, outgoing girl who loved to be the center of attention. "I've never really been insecure. I just skipped that. I've never been shy," she noted. "I hated clothes when I was little. When I was, like, four, I'd run around the neighborhood naked."[5] Clarkson thinks her confidence came from being born and raised in Texas. "My stepdad ... will talk to the girl who delivers the pizza for an hour. I was just raised like that," she explained. "I'm from Texas and that's what we're like."[6]

Kelly loved to perform as a child and used to sing songs from Walt Disney musicals, such as Beauty and the Beast, for her friends and family.

Kelly loved to perform and entertain people from an early age, and she persuaded several of her childhood friends to play along with her favorite games. One of her friends, Ashley Donovan, kept a karaoke machine in her closet and put a sign on the door that read "Kelly's Recording Studio." Kelly spent a great deal of time in the closet, belting out popular songs while Ashley sat by listening.

Kelly also loved to sing the theme songs from Walt Disney musicals such as *Beauty and the Beast* and *The Little Mermaid* for her friends and family. Kelly and another childhood friend often produced their own shows in the living room. "Me and my friend Amber Gibson, when I was little, used to make up dances every hour," she remembered. "And we'd be like, 'OK, Mom, you have to watch,' and we'd drag people into the living room to be our audience. I never really thought about whether they liked it; I just wanted them to watch."[7]

Singing in School

In 1995, Kelly was given an opportunity to perform beyond her family's living room. Cindy Glenn, a music teacher at Pauline Hughes Middle School, heard Kelly singing in the hallway. Recognizing the seventh grader's natural talent, Glenn invited her to join the school choir. Although Kelly had never had singing lessons, she soon demonstrated a remarkable vocal range. She could move easily from singing low notes to high notes and back again, and she could adapt her voice to a wide variety of musical styles.

Shortly after she joined the choir, Kelly was asked to perform a solo at a school assembly. She sang "Vision of Love"—a song made famous by pop star Mariah Carey—and received a standing ovation. From that moment on, Kelly knew that she wanted to become a professional singer. "Singing gave me confidence," she said.

Friends at school were nervous because they didn't know what they wanted to do with the rest of their lives, but I had a peaceful feeling inside because I knew. I knew that I would make a living at this since a seventh-grade assembly, when I was about to go out and sing a Mariah Carey song in front of the whole town. Other singers were throwing up out of fear but I wasn't afraid at all. Singing just seemed a natural thing.[8]

After her success at the junior high assembly, Kelly continued to sing in the choir as a student at Burleson High School. She also played on the varsity volleyball team and starred in several school musicals, including *Seven Brides for Seven Brothers* and *Brigadoon*. After graduating from high school in 2000, Kelly decided not to go to college. Instead, she was determined to follow her dream of becoming a professional singer. "I didn't want to go to college. My goal was to be a major recording artist," she explained. "And when I told my mom, she never once discouraged me. She said, 'Kelly, you can do it!'"[9]

Giving Up on an Early Ambition

Although she enjoyed performing from an early age, Kelly Clarkson did not always dream of becoming a professional singer. In fact, her first career goal was to study and care for sea creatures as a marine biologist. This childhood ambition ended in a hurry, however, when Kelly saw the movie *Jaws*. This blockbuster hit from 1975 features a great white shark that terrorizes the residents of a New England resort town. "I did really want to become a marine biologist, but then I saw *Jaws*, and had second thoughts," she recalled. "I remember someone telling me that sharks only attack in their own territory, and I thought to myself, 'Yeah, like the water!' and I left that dream right there!"

Quoted in Terrina Hussein, "From Country Girl to Pop Star," *Asia Africa Intelligence Wire*, February 19, 2005.

Kelly Clarkson's mom, Jeanne, always supported her daughter's dream of becoming a professional singer.

Hoping for a Break

After graduating from high school, Clarkson spent the next two years struggling to break into the music business. She wrote original songs and recorded herself singing them. She sent these demo tapes off to record companies in the hope of being discovered. "I was sending out demos, getting doors slammed in my face,"[10] she remembered. Clarkson understood that she was one of thousands of talented girls across the country looking for a big break, but the support of her family and friends kept her from feeling discouraged.

Clarkson's talent attracted some attention from recording industry executives. In fact, she received two offers of recording contracts. However, in both cases, Clarkson turned the offers down because the record companies wanted to make fundamental changes to her style. "One record label wanted me to make nothing but bubblegum pop music, and the other wanted me to dye my hair blonde and be someone I wasn't, so that didn't work out at all!"[11] she recalled. "I was confident enough that something better would come along."[12]

While she was trying to build a career as a singer, Clarkson supported herself by taking a series of odd jobs in her hometown. She worked as a cocktail waitress at a local comedy club, as a clerk in a bookstore and a pharmacy, and as a ticket seller in a movie theater. Through hard work and determination, Clarkson eventually saved enough money to help her to follow her dream to Los Angeles, California—the heart of the American entertainment industry.

Facing Disappointment

In late 2001, Clarkson moved to Los Angeles hoping to meet and impress influential people in the entertainment industry. She lived with a friend in a small rental apartment off Melrose Avenue. For the next four months, Clarkson went to auditions for both singing jobs and acting roles. She was willing to take any opportunity to appear in front of a live audience and begin to make a name for herself in show business.

Kelly worked briefly with well-known songwriter Gerry Goffin, right, who wanted to feature Clarkson as a backup singer.

One of Clarkson's first professional appearances came when she was hired as an extra for the ABC-TV series *Sabrina, the Teenage Witch*. Clarkson was paid about $70 per day to be one of the people in the background in scenes where the main characters went out in public. Clarkson also appeared as an extra on the comedy series *That '70s Show* and *Dharma & Greg*, and she played a small role in the 2002 film *Issues 101*.

During her stay in Los Angeles, Clarkson also auditioned for roles as a backup singer for various recording artists. She found these experiences frustrating and disappointing. Although several producers expressed appreciation for her strong voice, they all rejected her because they did not like her singing style or appearance. One person told her she needed to lose weight, for example, and another said her soulful singing made her sound "too black."

Then Clarkson thought she had found a promising path to a recording career when she began working with the well-known songwriter Gerry Goffin. During the 1960s and 1970s, Goffin had collaborated with singer Carole King to write hit songs such as "(You Make Me Feel Like) A Natural Woman" and "Up on the Roof." Goffin told Clarkson he was planning to record an album of new songs and wanted to feature her as a backup singer. Although the association with Goffin gave Clarkson some valuable on-the-job training in songwriting and recording techniques, the project was put on hold when Goffin developed a serious illness.

Cutting Her Losses

After this professional disappointment, Clarkson also suffered a personal loss when her Los Angeles apartment burned down, destroying all her possessions. Clarkson hung on to her dream for a few more days by sleeping in her car and taking showers at a gym. She quickly ran out of money, however, and was forced to return to Texas. "My apartment burned down during a time when I was being screwed over by a lot of industry people,"[13] she noted. "I decided to cut my losses and go home."[14]

When she returned to Burleson, Clarkson felt disappointed that her move to Los Angeles had not resulted in a big break, but she still remained determined to launch a career as a singer. While she considered her next move, Clarkson got a job promoting the energy drink Red Bull. She drove around in a car that had a giant can of Red Bull on top, and she handed out free samples of the product at local bars and popular hangouts like Joe Pool Lake.

Chapter 2

Becoming the First American Idol

A fter her best efforts resulted in a series of disappointments, Kelly Clarkson finally broke into the music business in an unexpected way. In 2002, she became a contestant on the hit reality-TV singing competition *American Idol*. Each week, Clarkson impressed the judges and won the hearts of viewers with her strong voice and appealing stage presence. At the end of the season, she was selected as the winner of a million-dollar recording contract.

Getting Valuable Support from Friends

When Clarkson returned home from Los Angeles in the spring of 2002, she remained determined to become a professional singer. But because her efforts to launch a career in music had resulted in so many disappointments, she was not sure what to do next. Luckily for Clarkson, some of her friends came up with an exciting idea.

Just a few days after she got back to Burleson, Clarkson went to visit her friends Jessica and Halie Brake. The girls' mother, Terry, had heard an advertisement on the radio inviting singers to audition for spots on an upcoming television program. Terry showed the girls an Internet site describing the new program, which was called *American Idol: The Search for a Superstar*.

Kelly's hometown friends supported her career ambitions and filled the Burleson High gymnasium to show their support during the American Idol *finale.*

The auditions were being held in several cities across the United States, including nearby Dallas.

Knowing that Clarkson had a powerful singing voice, the Brakes encouraged her to attend the auditions. "We always knew she could sing," Terry noted. "We just didn't know how or where she'd get the big chance."[15] When Clarkson expressed doubts about the idea—claiming that she was not pretty enough or thin enough to win a televised singing competition—the Brakes convinced her to take a chance. "We told her, 'Just be yourself. If you show you're kind of silly and sweet, they'll love you,"[16] Halie recalled. Jessica even filled out the online application for Clarkson.

Auditioning for *American Idol*

As the date of the audition approached, Clarkson grew more and more hopeful that it might provide a path to success in the music business. In fact, she became so excited about the audition that she could not sleep the night before. Always known for being a heavy sleeper, Clarkson did not want to risk oversleeping and missing her chance to appear on *American Idol*. Her solution to this problem was to stay up all night. She ended up going to the Brakes' house at four in the morning to seek her friends' help in staying awake.

When Clarkson showed up a few hours later at the Wyndham Anatole Hotel in Dallas, she joined thousands of other young singers who hoped to land a spot on the new reality TV series. *American Idol* was based on a hit British television program called *Pop Idol*. In both shows, amateur singers between the ages of sixteen and twenty-four auditioned for a chance to showcase their talents on TV. After a series of callbacks and elimination rounds, the top ten finalists were selected to appear on the show. These contestants sang songs in a different style each week, and their performances were reviewed by a panel of judges. At the end of each episode, TV viewers were asked to call in and vote for their favorite performers. The most popular contestants advanced to the next round, while the least popular were eliminated from the competition. At the end of the season, the overall winner received a million-dollar recording contract.

At the initial auditions for *American Idol*, Clarkson and the other hopefuls were each asked to sing a favorite song without accompaniment for one minute. Clarkson sang "At Last," a soulful ballad that was written by the bandleader Glenn Miller.

American Idol *was based on the hit British television*
program **Pop Idol.**

The three judges—British recording industry executive Simon
Cowell, former pop singer Paula Abdul, and music producer
Randy Jackson—praised her performance and voted unani-
mously to send her into the next round of the competition.
Nevertheless, Cowell claimed that Clarkson's original audition
was not particularly memorable. "There wasn't anything about
her that jumped out at us at that point," he recalled. "She was
just a girl with a good voice."[17]

Still, Clarkson did much better than most of the 10,000
people across the country who auditioned for the show. Although
a few of the young singers stood out as talented performers,
many other hopefuls sang painfully off-key and were ridiculed

Every year, thousands of amateur singers between the ages of sixteen and twenty-four audition for a spot on American Idol.

by the judges. Highlights from the early rounds of auditions, with their mix of impressive and terrible singers, became one of the most popular features of *American Idol*.

Advancing to the Top Ten

Following her original audition in Dallas, Clarkson was invited to a series of callbacks that narrowed the field of contestants to 120. These contestants were offered a trip to Hollywood, California, where they attended two more rounds of auditions. Clarkson continued to perform well, singing songs like Aretha Franklin's "Respect," Dionne Warwick's "I Say a Little Prayer," and Vanessa Williams's "Save the Best for Last." As more and more of the other singers were eliminated, Clarkson reached the top thirty finalists who were given the opportunity to appear on television.

American Idol made its premiere on the Fox television network on June 11, 2002, and the show quickly became the surprise hit of the summer. Since there was only time for ten contestants to sing in each hour-long episode, Clarkson did not perform on the air until two weeks later. She decided to sing "Respect," the classic Motown tune that had helped make Aretha Franklin a superstar. "I wasn't on the first two shows and I thought I would have to come out with a big song," Clarkson explained. "I had sung 'Respect' karaoke with friends. I feel that song and I love that song. It's upbeat, it's got soul, it shows your range. It's a show-stopper, the song itself."[18]

Clarkson's version of "Respect" impressed both the judges and TV viewers, who voted to make her one of the ten finalists who would compete to become the first American Idol. Clarkson and the other finalists then moved into a thirteen-bedroom, eight-bathroom mansion on Mulholland Drive, overlooking Los Angeles. The luxurious estate featured a pool, hot tub, workout room, and chef. Unfortunately for Clarkson, her busy schedule of promotional appearances, rehearsals, voice coaching, and wardrobe selection left her very little time to enjoy her sur-roundings. "The stress level of learning songs and performing them live on television is huge," acknowledged *American Idol*

Clarkson's performances often impressed the usually critical **American Idol** *judges, (from left) Randy Jackson, Paula Abdul, and Simon Cowell.*

executive producer Nigel Lythgoe. "Most artists never do that in a lifetime."[19]

Despite the grueling schedule and pressure-packed atmosphere of the competition, however, Clarkson claimed that she and the other finalists got along well during the taping of the show. "Of course, there are going to be ups and downs with people because of the stress, but nobody got in fights," she recalled. "We were all too busy. Nobody believes us, but we were literally too busy to have any kind of conflict."[20]

Standing Out from the Competition

As the competition continued, Clarkson and the other finalists performed a new song each week. They chose most of the songs themselves, although sometimes their selection was limited by the theme assigned given to an episode of the show. One week the contestants had to sing Motown songs, for example, while other weeks featured love songs, Big Band tunes, or songs from a certain decade. Regardless of the theme, Clarkson consistently chose soulful ballads made famous by some of the most powerful voices in the music industry. She sang Diana Ross's "All I Need" for Motown week, Aretha Franklin's "(You Make Me Feel Like) A Natural Woman" for 1960s week, Dionne Warwick's "Walk on By" for love song week, and Celine Dion's "I Surrender" for 1980s/1990s week.

While most of the other finalists experienced ups and downs, Clarkson's performances were given mostly positive reviews from Cowell, Abdul, and Jackson. In fact, one writer claimed that the range and power of Clarkson's voice was "a constant source of awe to *Idol*'s trio of feuding judges"[21] throughout the competition. While her rivals were being eliminated one by one, Clarkson remained humble about her talent. "I know my voice and what I can do," she stated. "I just rehearse and pray to God that He won't let me screw up on national television."[22]

As well as her impressive voice, Clarkson's friendly, down-to-earth personality was popular with fans of the show. According to *American Idol* host Ryan Seacrest, Clarkson gained many admirers with her "candid, cute, bubbly charisma and charm."[23] As a reviewer who watched the taping of an episode with a live audience noted,

> Of all the contestants, Clarkson seemed to be enjoying herself the most. Her talent is natural and she has fun, a highly underrated quality. The power of her voice sent chills, and … it felt like everyone, as if they were sitting in a bar, wanted to sing along with her.[24]

Clarkson also stood out from some of her competitors because of her modest, understated look. Instead of wearing tight, sexy

American Idol Judge Simon Cowell

Simon Cowell, the acid-tongued British judge known for his blunt—but usually accurate—criticisms of contestants' performances, is one of the most popular aspects of *American Idol*. Known as "Mr. Nasty," Cowell bases his assessments on a long and successful career in the music industry.

The son of a music executive, Cowell was born on October 7, 1959, in London, England. After dropping out of school when he was seventeen, Cowell took a job in the mailroom at EMI Music Publishing. He quickly moved up through the ranks and proved himself to be a good judge of singing talent. Cowell later moved to music giant BMG and set up his own record label, S Records, which signed up a number of well-known pop groups. In fact, between 1997 and 2002 Cowell's label was responsible for artists that sold more than 25 million albums and produced seventeen number one songs.

In 2001, Cowell joined forces with fellow entertainment executive Simon Fuller to create *Pop Idol*, a British TV show in which young, unknown singers competed to win a successful recording contract. Cowell appeared on the show as one of the judges and received a great deal of attention for his harsh criticisms of contestants' performances.

The following year, Cowell starred in the U.S. version of the show, *American Idol*. Adding to his reputation as one of television's favorite villains, he told various contestants that their singing was "pathetic" or "rubbish." Cowell refused to apologize for his critical words, claiming that he was just doing his job. "My only objective is to find a great singer who is going to sell millions of records for my label," he explained in *People*. "If you get called a few names, well—tough luck, you know? I'll live with that."

Julie K.L. Dam and Alexis Chiu, "Judge Dread," *People*, July 8, 2002, p. 107.

American Idol judge Simon Cowell.

clothing favored by most pop stars, she often performed on the show wearing sophisticated evening gowns. "I just try to be as real as I can be, the kind of person who doesn't really care if she is caught without makeup, not some ultra-professional musician who is only 'on' when in front of the camera,"[25] she explained.

Becoming a Finalist

By mid-August, six of the ten finalists had been eliminated from *American Idol*, leaving only Clarkson, Tamyra Gray, Justin Guarini, and Nikki McKibbin to compete for the grand prize.

The other talented finalists of American Idol were often stiff competition for Clarkson.

Rating the *American Idol* Judges

During the first season of *American Idol*, the show's three judges—Paula Abdul, Simon Cowell, and Randy Jackson—received nearly as much public interest and media attention as the contestants. Each week, fans and reviewers analyzed the judges' comments, compared their styles and preferences, and shared information about their backgrounds and personalities. "Abdul tends to give out warm fuzzies; Jackson is hit-or-miss in giving a direct assessment but generally forgiving of minor slips; Cowell tells it like it is," Phil Gallo wrote in *Daily Variety*.

Immediately after Clarkson's victory on *American Idol*, many interviewers asked for her opinions about the judges. They were particularly interested to hear what she had to say about Simon Cowell, the British recording executive whose harsh criticism sometimes brought contestants to the verge of tears. "Simon fills his purpose," she told the *Sunday Mirror*. "He informs the performers and the audience at home that the music industry is tough and not everyone will love you. He gives it to you straight. Sometimes he's wrong—like all critics—but he's so charming and clever he makes it acceptable."

Although Clarkson enjoyed working with singer and choreographer Paula Abdul, she admitted that Randy Jackson was her favorite judge. She showed her respect for his range of experiences in the music industry as a bass player and record producer. Throughout the competition, Clarkson always tried to remain calm and avoid getting too excited, or too disappointed, by the judges' comments. "It's three people's opinion," she stated. "There are a lot more people in the industry."

"Fashion: An American Life; In the U.S., *American Idol* Winner Kelly Clarkson Is a Diva in the Making," *Sunday Mirror*, September 7, 2003, p. 14; Phil Gallo, "*American Idol: The Search for a Superstar*," *Daily Variety*, August 20, 2002, p. 5.

Many people predicted that the competition would come down to Clarkson and Gray, who were widely considered to have the strongest voices among the remaining contestants. Gray was clearly the favorite of Cowell, who described her performances as "as close to perfection as you could possibly get"[26] and openly encouraged viewers to vote for her. He and millions of television viewers were shocked, therefore, when Gray became the next contestant to be eliminated.

The following week, the top three contestants each sang two songs that were selected by the judges. Clarkson sang Celine Dion's "Think Twice" and Mariah Carey's "Without You." Once again, her performances wowed the judges, and she advanced to the final round. McKibbin ended up being eliminated on the basis of viewer votes, so Clarkson faced off against Guarini in the season finale. Despite the pressure of performing in the finale, Clarkson insisted that she felt no animosity toward her rival. "It's not a competition between the contestants," she stated. "It's me competing with myself."[27]

As the season finale of *American Idol* approached, most people argued that Clarkson had a stronger singing voice than her rival. Still, few people were willing to count Guarini out. The curly-haired native of Doylestown, Pennsylvania, had a strong stage presence, and his good looks and pleasant manner had helped him develop a large fan base among young, female viewers of the show. "Justin Guarini definitely has the 'X' factor," noted one reviewer. "Sexy and smooth, he [comes] across as the real deal."[28]

Winning the Crown

In the final competition, Clarkson and Guarini each performed three songs. Of these songs, two were written specifically for the show, "A Moment Like This" and "Before Your Love." After singing these two songs back-to-back, the two finalists were allowed to perform a song of their choice that they had sung earlier in the competition. Clarkson chose "Respect," while Guarini sang "Get Here." With these songs, TV viewers had the

American Idol finalists Justin Guarini and Kelly Clarkson sing together during the final episode, which scored over 22 million television viewers.

opportunity to compare and contrast the two contestants, and the votes were tallied immediately afterward.

The results of the *American Idol* competition were announced the following night, September 4, at the end of a special two-hour episode. Nearly 23 million people across the country tuned in to find out who won. It turned out to be Clarkson, who received 58 percent of the 15.5 million votes cast. Guarini accepted his defeat graciously, giving Clarkson a big hug and proclaiming, "No one deserves it more than this woman."[29]

When she heard the results, a delighted Clarkson cried tears of joy. The tears continued streaming down her face as she performed the inspirational ballad that had been written for

Over 8 million television viewers voted for Clarkson to win
American Idol.

the winner of the show, "A Moment Like This." The other nine finalists eventually joined her on stage to help her finish the song. Clarkson found the whole experience a bit overwhelming. "I was so exhausted from the competition I didn't know I was crying until I watched a tape of the final show a few weeks later," she recalled. "Isn't that funny? I don't remember a bit of it."[30]

Even after her victory had a chance to sink in, Clarkson still had trouble believing it had happened. "Throughout the whole competition, I wasn't looking to win; I was looking for exposure," she explained. "I'm just an average girl, so I never expect the top. I never look that far in advance."[31]

Chapter 3

Getting Caught in the Whirlwind

After becoming the first winner of *American Idol*, Kelly Clarkson was swept up in a whirlwind of publicity. She was thrilled to have finally achieved her dream of becoming a professional singer, and she enjoyed many aspects of her instant fame. Over the course of the next year, however, Clarkson found herself struggling to control the direction of her music career.

Breaking Records with Her First Single

As the winner of *American Idol*, Clarkson received the grand prize of a million-dollar recording contract with RCA Records. Her first single—featuring the two songs that were written especially for the show, "A Moment Like This" and "Before Your Love"—was released on September 17, 2002. After making its debut at number 52 on *Billboard* magazine's Top 100 chart, it sold a remarkable 236,000 copies in its first week of release to jump all the way to the number one position. With this, Clarkson broke a longstanding record that had been set by the Beatles for the biggest jump in *Billboard* chart history.

As well as recording the hit single, Clarkson was also required to make many public appearances in the weeks following her

After winning American Idol, Kelly appeared on several talk shows, including "The Tonight Show with Jay Leno," to promote her album.

victory on *American Idol.* The show's producers wanted to capitalize on her popularity to generate sales of her record and to increase interest in future seasons of *American Idol.* As a result, Clarkson performed songs on a number of TV talk shows and gave several interviews on the radio. She was also featured in countless articles in newspapers across the country, and her image graced the covers of several major magazines. The cable TV music channel VH-1 even produced a documentary about her life.

Following the success of *American Idol,* the Fox network televised a concert special featuring Clarkson and the other twenty-nine finalists who had competed for spots on the show. The concert was broadcast live from the MGM-Grand Hotel in Las Vegas on September 23. A few weeks later, Clarkson's music video for "A Moment Like This" made its debut on the cable music channel MTV. Filmed in an old, abandoned theater, the video also featured footage of Clarkson's emotional victory on *American Idol.*

Clarkson's hectic schedule continued in October, when she embarked on a six-week, thirty-city national concert tour with the top ten *Idol* contestants. Clarkson also sang four songs on *American Idol Greatest Moments*, a compilation CD of music by the show's ten finalists. In addition to the two tracks from her single,

Kelly was able to perform with one of her idols, country singer Reba McEntire, during the show "American Idol in Vegas" in 2002.

"R-E-S-P-E-C-T"

Kelly Clarkson distinguished herself from the competition on *American Idol* by singing "Respect," a rock-and-roll classic with a powerful message. *Detroit Free Press* music writer Kelley L. Carter described the song as "one of the most influential recordings in pop music history and one of the most indelible songs to come out of the rock and roll era."

When Clarkson performed "Respect" during her first appearance on *American Idol*, it earned her a spot in the top ten. She sang the song again during the finals, and it helped her defeat rival Justin Guarini to win the million-dollar recording contract. Clarkson explained that she had always appreciated the spirit of the song, as well as its influential place in music history.

Written by Otis Redding in 1965, "Respect" became famous two years later, when Motown legend Aretha Franklin recorded her own funky, aggressive version. Franklin's single came out in June 1967, a time when African Americans were demanding equal rights and opportunities in society through the civil rights movement. That summer, in fact, civil rights protests and violent race riots took place in Detroit and other cities across the United States.

Against this historical backdrop, many people came to associate "Respect" with the African American struggle for civil rights. "When Aretha came out with 'Respect,' we weren't getting any respect. Black folks were being disrespected, being beat down, killed trying to get the right to vote," remembered civil rights leader Benjamin Chavis. "So when she came out with this song, 'Respect,' it was like she was fulfilling not only an urgency of the movement of that time, but she made known through her song that we were going to get respect."

Kelley L. Carter, "40 Years of 'Respect,'" *Detroit Free Press*, June 3, 2007, p. A1.

Clarkson also performed "Respect" and "(You Make Me Feel Like) A Natural Woman." She also joined the rest of the finalists in a group rendition of "California Dreamin'."

Facing a Backlash

Although Clarkson's record-breaking single sales and hectic publicity schedule made lots of headlines in the fall of 2002, many people in the entertainment industry expected her fame to be short-lived. They thought that the popularity of *American Idol* would fade quickly from the public eye and that Clarkson's singing career would be over as quickly as it had begun. After all, reality-based television programs like *Survivor*, *The Bachelor*, and *The Amazing Race* had already turned dozens of ordinary Americans into instant celebrities, but none of those people had managed to turn their success on reality TV into a lasting career.

On the other hand, some analysts claimed that *American Idol* had more in common with the talent shows that were popular in the early decades of TV history than with modern reality TV programs. "For the most part, we have always had some original amateur hour. It has always been a viable format for Americans. It's just a matter of adapting it for the times,"[32] said Ron Simon, curator of the Museum of Radio and Records. These shows produced a number of singers who went on to become big stars, including Frank Sinatra and Gladys Knight.

Despite these historical examples, however, some people in the music industry rejected Clarkson's talent simply because it was discovered on *American Idol*. They believed that her popularity stemmed from her association with the show, rather than from a true appreciation for her artistic gifts. "For many in the music business, *Idol* is the starkest example of how marketing concepts seem to have trumped art," noted one critic. "Some analysts have said the show's appeal stems more from the drama of competition and the judges' critiques than it does from the music."[33]

This criticism of Clarkson and *American Idol* created some uncomfortable situations for the young singer. Shortly after her victory, for example, Clarkson received an invitation from a national youth organization, Champions of Hope, to sing the national anthem at a ceremony honoring the anniversary of the September 11 terrorist attacks. Many people complained

Clarkson faced criticism in the aftermath of Idol from people who felt the show—and her talent—was manufactured.

that it was inappropriate for Clarkson to perform during a national day of mourning, because they felt that her appearance would promote *American Idol.* Clarkson considered dropping out because she did not want to create hard feelings, but she eventually decided to honor her commitment to appear at the event.

Much of the criticism Clarkson faced immediately following her victory centered around her top-selling single. Many critics attributed the popularity of the recording to its connection with the TV show. They claimed that "A Moment Like This" and "Before Your Love"— despite all of the national radio airplay they received—were inferior songs that were not well suited to Clarkson's voice. They warned that she and her managers needed to come up with significantly better material for her first album. "Celine Dion or Mariah Carey wouldn't cross the street to spit on those songs. And that's who Kelly is competing against now—it's not just Justin anymore," wrote *Rolling Stone* music editor Joe Levy. "People voted for Kelly because she had a sweetness and a vulnerability in addition to astounding ability. They've got to give her songs that communicate something about her personality. Otherwise, she might well be queen of the Thanksgiving Day parade rather than a pop star."[34]

Answering Her Critics

Clarkson often faced criticism in the months following her victory on *American Idol.* Many interviewers asked her to comment on the quality of her hit single, for example, and to assess whether its popularity was linked to the success of the show. "'A Moment Like This' wouldn't have been anything without the show's meaning. It fit the show perfectly; that's why it sold," she acknowledged. "Now, to say it suits my style? No. If I were to choose my first single coming out on my own, that wouldn't have been it."[35]

While people were debating whether Clarkson was a talented artist or simply a product of *American Idol,* Clarkson insisted that she and the other contestants had showcased their individual abilities and personalities on the program. She argued that TV viewers had chosen her as the winner of the competition on the basis of her performances. She also emphasized that she—rather than the show's producers—had been responsible for those performances by making all of the important decisions regarding songs, arrangements, and wardrobe. "There are going to be people, until the day I die, who are going to say, 'Oh, she's the product of a TV show.' To some extent that's true. On the other hand, we made the show—so who's the product?" she noted. "It's funny to me whenever people use the words 'puppet' and 'manufactured.' It's the exact opposite. I went on the show. I sang what I wanted. I wore what I wanted. I said what I wanted."[36]

Clarkson ultimately chose to ignore the critics who questioned whether winning a TV singing competition would provide her with a path to lasting stardom. She was thrilled to have finally gotten her big break, and she was determined to make the most of the opportunity. "Any artist is going to accept whatever comes their way," she declared. "They're not going to say, 'No way, I'm not going to go on this hit television show. I want to go the hard route.'"[37]

Clarkson recognized that the fame she had gained as the winner of *American Idol* would not last long. Although the show had provided her with a great deal of exposure among music-industry executives and record-buying fans, she realized that she needed to turn the opportunity into a successful career. "She never once had to be told that she was going to have to keep waking up every day and proving herself," said an RCA executive. "Despite all of her sudden fame, she knew what it took to break a record and establish a career: not just one television show, but constant promotion and constant performing."[38]

Fighting for Control

During all this publicity and media attention, Clarkson started working on her debut album. Executives at RCA Records pushed her to finish the recording sessions very quickly. They

Clarkson responded to critics by performing live often to show her skills, and insisted in interviews that her performances, clothing decisions, and behavior on the show were genuine.

wanted to release the CD in November 2002 to take advantage of her popularity and to increase record sales at Christmas. "Performers who appeal to that teenage demographic can come and go so rapidly," concert promoter Jerry Thompson explained. "That demographic just turns on to its likes and dislikes a day at a time."[39]

Representatives of the record label believed that timing would be an important factor in the album's success, so they recruited a number of well-known songwriters to supply material for it. They also arranged for Clarkson to work with Clive Davis, a legendary record producer and the head of RCA Records.

Shortly after beginning work on the album, Clarkson asked Davis to let her record some of the songs she had written over the years. She felt that the album would only reflect her personality, interests, and musical style if she were allowed to contribute original songs to it. "I'm all about my sound and my style," she stated. "That's important for me to stand up to. I came out on the show being myself and doing what I like, and people voted for me. So I already have a fan base based on what I like and what I do."[40]

Unfortunately for Clarkson, Davis and other RCA executives resisted the idea of letting her write songs for the album. They argued that Clarkson had won over fans by using her powerful voice to interpret the work of other artists. Since she had never demonstrated her talents as a songwriter, they wanted established musicians to compose the songs for her first album. But Clarkson was determined to make an album that reflected her unique talents and tastes, even if it meant delaying the CD's release by several months. "Basically people right off the show said, 'Of course her CD is gonna do good. She's got to strike while the iron is hot,'" she recalled. "I put my foot down and said, 'Nope, not gonna do that.' I kept going on my website and saying, 'Do you want it now or do you want quality?' I wanted to make a CD that was a representation of me, not a representation of the show."[41]

Clarkson and RCA eventually reached a compromise which gave her more time to create the album that she wanted. "I met with [*American Idol* producer] Simon [Fuller] and told

Clarkson worked with legendary record producer and head of RCA Records, Clive Davis.

him I couldn't put out a CD that soon. There was no way it could be a representation of me," Clarkson remembered. "He said, 'I understand perfectly. Let's wait until you get the right material.' So he was actually really cool about it, which I didn't know would happen."[42] Although many people in the music industry warned that delaying the release of Clarkson's album could have a negative impact on sales, RCA agreed to wait until the spring of 2003.

Releasing Another Successful Single

Clarkson's decision to delay the release of her debut album until she could find songs that suited her musical style proved to be a good one. While she continued to work on the CD, Clarkson released a second single, "Miss Independent," that marked a major musical departure from the ballads on her previous release. "I was the one who pushed the single," she explained. "I need people to know right away that I like rock, soul, groove, country, urban ... I don't want everyone to think my album is a bunch of ballads."[43]

"Miss Independent" was originally written by Christina Aguilera, but the pop star had left the song unfinished when it did not fit on one of her albums. Clarkson collaborated with veteran songwriter Rhett Lawrence to finish the song and adapt it to her personal style. The song's rock edge and assertive lyrics helped expand Clarkson's fan base beyond *American Idol* viewers to include a younger, hipper audience. "Miss Independent" reached the top ten on the *Billboard* charts and also earned Clarkson a Grammy Award nomination for Best Female Pop Vocal Performance of the Year.

Showing Her Range

The success of "Miss Independent"—as well as the contrast between its style and that of "A Moment Like This"—created a great deal of anticipation about the release of Clarkson's debut album. When *Thankful* finally came out in April 2003, it did not disappoint the singer's many fans. In addition to the tracks that had already been released as singles, the album included songs in a wide range of musical styles, from pop and rock to country and gospel. "I grew up with many different styles of music," Clarkson explained. "There's no way I'm going to limit myself ... I like rock. I like alternative. I like country. I like R&B [rhythm and blues]. I am going to keep it pretty versatile."[44]

Although Clarkson was not credited with the solo writing of any of the album's songs, she collaborated with well-known songwriters on several of the tracks. For example, she co-wrote the title track, "Thankful," with R&B star Kenneth "Babyface" Edmonds. Clarkson said that she wrote the song as a way to express her appreciation to everyone who had supported her career. "It's about my mom and my friends and fans and everybody I'm working with," she noted. "Knock on wood, I have the best luck working with people."[45]

Delaying the release date of her debut album did not seem to have a negative impact on sales. *Thankful* sold an impressive 297,000 copies in its first week of release to debut at number one on the *Billboard* charts. It went on to sell over 2 million copies by the end of the year and was certified double platinum by the Recording Industry Association of America. One reviewer claimed that the delay actually made the album more appealing to fans, because it gave Clarkson and Davis "time to figure out how to balance the expectations of people who wanted an *Idol* souvenir with those who demanded signs of artistic growth."[46]

Thankful also received mostly favorable reviews from music critics. Many reviewers praised the power and range of Clarkson's voice. "Her voice, at times raspy, at times beautifully sultry, is a potent reminder of why America embraced her," Henry Goldblatt wrote in *Entertainment Weekly*.

Clarkson glides through octaves with the masterful control of someone who's been doing this for decades. And her range is awesome: in a dozen tracks, she owns pop ("Just Missed the Train"), R&B ("Thankful"), country ("Low"), and gospel ("Anytime").[47]

Clarkson's album Thankful *sold over 2 million copies by the end of 2003 and was certified double platinum.*

On the other hand, some critics felt that the songs on *Thankful* showed too much variety. They claimed that the broad range of musical styles on the album made it difficult to show Clarkson's real personality. "Clarkson is sweet and has tons of talent, unlike some big-selling artists out there. Her voice is also strong, sexy, and mature, which is pretty amazing considering she's never had a professional voice lesson," Joanna Hensley wrote in the *Lafayette Journal and Courier*.

> But her versatility is also the album's major downfall. One minute she sounds like Christina Aguilera; the next moment she sounds like Sheryl Crow or Faith Hill. And while it's great to pander to several genres, it's also hard to find a niche with fans when you're obviously trying to sound like every other star.[48]

Acting in a Clunker

While Clarkson's first album was given mostly positive reviews, most critics did not like her first movie role. As part of a business deal Clarkson made following her victory on *American Idol*, she had agreed to co-star with Justin Guarini in a musical love story called *From Justin to Kelly*. *Idol* creator Simon Fuller rushed the movie through production to take advantage of the popularity the two young singers had gained from their appearance on the show. The movie was filmed in Miami over six weeks and released in June 2003.

Clarkson had misgivings about the film from the beginning. She disliked the story—in which a girl from Texas meets and falls in love with a boy from Pennsylvania while on spring break in Florida—and also expressed doubts about her own acting ability. "I knew when I read the script it was going to be real, real bad, but when I won, I signed that piece of paper, and I could not get out of it," she explained. "Seriously, I never thought I could act, but I knew I could sing. Not to sound cocky, but I can!"[49]

The movie From Justin to Kelly, *starring Idol finalists Kelly Clarkson and Justin Guarini bombed at the box office and received scathing reviews from critics.*

Kelly and Justin: Just Friends

From the time that Kelly Clarkson and Justin Guarini emerged as the two final contestants on *American Idol*, fans of both singers wondered about the nature of their personal relationship. Although each expressed fondness and respect for the other throughout the competition, they both insisted that they were just good friends. In fact, Clarkson and Guarini both compared their playful, supportive relationship to one that might exist between a brother and sister. They also claimed that the show and its aftermath kept them far too busy to have time for a boyfriend or girlfriend.

Despite their protests, however, the tabloids remained full of rumors about a romance between the two singers once they wrapped up *American Idol*. Interest in the couple peaked during the filming of their romantic beach movie, *From Justin to Kelly*, in the spring of 2003. At one point, Clarkson and Guarini were the center of so much celebrity gossip that "My mom called up and joked, 'I'm so mad I didn't get a wedding invitation!'" Clarkson recalled. The rumors finally started to die down after the movie came out and both singers moved on to other projects.

Jason Lynch, "From Idol to Star?" *People Weekly*, April 23, 2003, p. 71.

Unfortunately for Clarkson, her predictions about the film's quality turned out to be true. *From Justin to Kelly* bombed at the box office, earning only $5 million—or less than half of what it had cost to make. It also received scathing reviews from movie critics, who complained about the predictable plot, silly song and dance routines, and poor acting performances. In a review for the *New York Times*, for example, Stephen Holden wrote that Clarkson and Guarini "go through their paces like dutiful puppets, lip-synching and strenuously aerobicizing in the beach

Rumors circulated about the nature of the relationship between Justin and Kelly.

party dance sequences to numbers that run from sanitized rap to the strawberry sundae froth of several billowing love songs."[50] Several Internet polls ranked the movie among the worst films ever made.

From Justin to Kelly received so much bad press that some people worried it might harm Clarkson's singing career, which had looked so promising a few months earlier with the success of her first album. But Clarkson kept her head up, viewed the situation with a sense of humor, and refused to allow one bad decision to define her career. "I don't believe I'm a 15-minute artist," she declared. "I'm in this for the long run."[51]

Staying Busy

Clarkson soon put the unsuccessful movie role behind her and immersed herself in other projects. In September 2003, she made a guest appearance on the NBC television series *American Dreams*. Set in the 1960s, the show often featured musical performances, with modern-day singers portraying artists who were popular during that time. The producers of the show allowed Clarkson to choose from among several performers from the 1960s. She decided to portray Brenda Lee—one of her mother's favorite singers—performing her hit song "Sweet Nothin's." Clarkson enjoyed appearing on *American Dreams* and introducing Lee's music to modern TV audiences. "I had seen the show right when it started up and I thought it would be a great idea to do it one day, and then the opportunity came up, and I thought, why not?"[52]

Clarkson returned to television in December 2003 as a contestant on *World Idol*. This international singing competition featured the winners of *Idol* shows from various countries, including Australia, Belgium, Canada, Poland, and South Africa. Clarkson entered the competition as the best-known contestant and was widely considered the favorite to win. She delivered a strong performance of "(You Make Me Feel Like) A Natural Woman" in the finals, but she finished second behind *Norwegian Idol* winner Kurt Nilsen. Afterward, Clarkson came under criticism in the international media for leaving without granting interviews or congratulating Nilsen. Clarkson defended her actions by saying that she had felt ill during the taping of the final show and needed to return to her hotel immediately.

Chapter 4

Breaking Away

After making a few questionable moves in the year after her victory on *American Idol*, Kelly Clarkson decided to take greater control over her career. She distanced herself from the show, wrote more of her own material, and developed more of a rock-style. As a result of these decisions, Clarkson became a mature, independent artist with the 2004 release of her second album, *Breakaway*.

Distancing Herself from *American Idol*

The whirlwind of publicity that had followed Clarkson's victory on *American Idol* finally began to subside in late 2003. Looking back over everything that had happened during the previous year—including the release of her first album and her first movie appearance—Clarkson acknowledged that her life had felt very hectic. "I think it hit so fast right off the bat that everything became normal really quickly so I didn't have time to think about it," she noted. "When you get thrown into a situation, you have to act. It's like, say there's a bad accident and all of a sudden you have to know what to do and be calm—and that's kind of what it was. I just got thrown into it."[53]

Many people within the music industry expressed admiration for the way in which Clarkson had handled her instant fame. Most people thought that she showed maturity and class in dealing with an intense, pressure-packed situation. "It's pretty heavy, what happened to her. She was thrown into the ocean

While she appreciated the exposure her career received from winning American Idol, Clarkson felt she needed to distance herself from the show to establish her own identity as an artist.

without a life preserver," said Clarkson's mentor, country music legend Reba McEntire. "And she handled it. I don't know that I could have."[54]

Even though she had handled the constant demands on her time with style, Clarkson was determined to take greater control over the future direction of her career. While she appreciated the exposure she had gained by winning *American Idol*, she felt that the time had come for her to begin distancing herself from the show. "I don't think I should hang onto the show, and I don't think the show should hang onto me,"[55] she explained. "The whole point of *American Idol* was for me to get a record deal and be able to make music that I love. People change and grow. My thing as an artist is to be limitless."[56]

Changing Her Sound

Clarkson found that her musical style and interests had changed after *American Idol*. While she continued to enjoy a wide variety of music, she increasingly found herself drawn toward a harder-edged, rock-based sound. She linked this development, in part, to performing with a live band during the concert tour for her first album. "I had never toured before making *Thankful*. I didn't know what kind of music was going to stick with me and hit home. But when I went on the road, these songs became more rock and less poppy," she remembered. "After touring, I figured out that's what I wanted to do."[57]

As well as gaining a greater understanding of her musical tastes, Clarkson also increased her knowledge of the music business in the year following *American Idol*. The experience of recording her first album gave her the confidence she needed to exert more control over her second album. "I had more experience being in a studio and working with major producers and

Clarkson's performances with a live band while on tour drew her towards a harder-edged, rock-based sound.

writers and so on," she noted. "I kind of came in and knew exactly what I wanted to do. I got to pick people who I wanted to work with."[58]

As she began working on *Breakaway*, her follow-up album to *Thankful*, Clarkson's biggest priority was to write as many songs for the album as possible. Once again, however, she faced resistance from Simon Fuller and his company, 19 Management. "To be totally honest, the problem was I wanted to write a lot of my own songs on *Breakaway*. Nobody else wanted me to. So there was this big ol' fight,"[59] Clarkson recalled. In order to get more creative control over the content of her second album, Clarkson ended her relationship with the management team that had guided her career since *American Idol*. Instead, she signed a contract with The Firm, a talent agency that represented many big names in the music business.

Releasing *Breakaway*

Clarkson's new management team was more supportive of her desire to write songs for her second album. Clarkson worked on *Breakaway* through much of 2004. Although she continued to work with well-known songwriters—including Max Martin, who had composed hit songs for Britney Spears and the Backstreet Boys; John Shanks, who had written for Sheryl Crow and Alanis Morissette; and former Evanescence guitar player Ben Moody—Clarkson was credited with the songwriting on six of the album's tracks.

When Clarkson's second album was finally released in December 2004, it immediately shot up to the number three position on the *Billboard* album charts. It also received glowing reviews from music critics, many of whom felt that *Breakaway* compared favorably with *Thankful*. Several reviewers commented that the new album's rock-based sound seemed to reflect Clarkson's individual style more accurately. "This time, the Texas-born chanteuse digs deeper emotionally, and the songs … generally fit better with her upbeat, down-to-earth personality," wrote one critic. "Perhaps the greatest asset of *Breakaway*—whose title track plays like

Music Industry Executive Clive Davis

As the president of RCA Records, Clive Davis is one of the most powerful figures in the recording industry. Over the course of his forty-year career, he has become legendary for his ability to find and develop talented musicians.

Davis was born on April 4, 1932, in Brooklyn, New York. After graduating from New York University and Harvard Law School, he ended up working in the legal department of Columbia Records, a division of CBS. He loved the music industry and worked his way up to become president of Columbia Records in 1967.

In this position, Davis discovered and signed many newly emerging rock-and-roll artists. Some of the artists he introduced to American audiences include Janis Joplin, Santana, Bruce Springsteen, Chicago, and Pink Floyd. Although Davis doubled Columbia's market share within three years, he was fired in 1972 following a government investigation into the company's finances.

After leaving Columbia, Davis merged various record labels to form Arista Records. At Arista, Davis guided the careers of a range of talented musicians, including Whitney Houston, Aretha Franklin, Annie Lennox, Sean "Diddy" Combs, and The Grateful Dead. Following a series of disagreements with parent company BMG, he left the company in 2000. That same year, Davis joined the Rock and Roll Hall of Fame as a record producer.

In 2003, Davis became the head of RCA Records, the company that provides million-dollar recording contracts to *American Idol* winners. He took an active role in guiding Kelly Clarkson's early career and won a Grammy Award for his work as producer of her second album, *Breakaway*. In 2007, however, Davis and Clarkson publicly disagreed over the singer's decision to write all the songs on her third album, *My December*.

Clarkson's anthem, about a small-town girl going for it—is that she sounds more like herself, which allows her to move beyond the typical."[60]

Many critics also praised the quality and range of Clarkson's voice, which shone throughout the new album. "Miles away—and ahead—of her lean R&B-influenced debut, Clarkson shows attitude, has a little fun, and reminds us why her voice took it all in the first place,"[61] noted another reviewer.

Topping the Charts

Breakaway soon proved to be just as popular among radio listeners and record buyers as it was among critics. The album produced four singles that spent time at the top of the *Billboard* charts, including the huge hit "Since U Been Gone." In a review for *Billboard*, Chuck Taylor described the song as "an utterly ideal showcase for Clarkson. There's glorious tempo, enough edge to rattle the speakers, a relentless, big-game hook—and it's a huge leap forward for the entertainer as a more confident, ever-maturing vocalist."[62]

The title track from the album became another highly popular single. "Breakaway" was written by alternative rock star Avril Lavigne. Clarkson explained on her website that she chose to record it because "I could relate to that song. It describes how I got into the business, verbatim. I did grow up in a small town, I wanted to get out, I felt like there was something … not better for me, but something different for me."[63] Clarkson's version of the song appeared on the soundtrack for the movie *The Princess Diaries 2: Royal Engagement*. She also sang "Breakaway" and "Since U Been Gone" during her time as the musical guest on *Saturday Night Live*.

Another single from the album that reached the top of the charts was one of Clarkson's original compositions, "Behind These Hazel Eyes." The singer said that she wrote the song to express her feelings about breaking up with a boyfriend. Taylor praised the tune in *Billboard*, writing that "Clarkson simply delivers a loose, tour-de-force vocal that simmers alongside a steroid-charged musical backdrop that is fun, fast, and furious."[64]

The other number-one hit to emerge from *Breakaway* was "Because of You," a song Clarkson wrote about her family. "It's about growing up in a broken home. My parents were together for seventeen years or so, and then all of a sudden, something went wrong," she explained on her website.

> If you see those things as a child, you see a family member cheating or people not trusting each other or people not communicating with each other, that affects you. You end up afraid to trust people, because you think you're going to get screwed over.[65]

The singer's fans seemed to connect with the emotions she expressed in the song.

Performing Live

With four chart-topping singles, *Breakaway* sold over 6 million copies to become the third-highest-selling album of 2005. The album's success meant that Clarkson found herself in constant demand to sing her hit songs in public. She accepted invitations to appear in televised concerts surrounding the NFL Super Bowl and NBA All-Star Game. Clarkson also launched a concert tour in the summer of 2005 to support the album.

In an effort to improve her live performance skills, Clarkson arranged for her Addicted Tour to play at smaller theaters across the country instead of at huge stadiums. Her live performances always reflected her decision to distance herself from *American Idol*. For example, she never performed "A Moment Like This," the ballad that had commemorated her victory on the show, and she only sang a few songs from *Thankful*. Clarkson's fans did not seem to mind the fact that she focused on more recent material, however, and her shows received many positive reviews. As a critic who attended one of Clarkson's concerts in California gushed, "So inspired was the performance, and so capable and impressive the vocals, it was easy to forget that Clarkson was discovered by a nationwide TV audience."[66]

Clarkson's album Breakaway, with it's pop-rock songs, became a huge success, producing several hit singles and the "Breakaway World Tour" in 2005.

The success of the songs on the Breakaway *album left Clarkson in constant demand to sing in public. She appeared on Saturday Night* Live *and concerts for the NFL Super Bowl and NBA All-Star Game.*

During the Addicted Tour, Clarkson found that she enjoyed performing her songs live and connecting with audiences "I love it," she noted. "I think it's a cool thing for the fans to get to know you better, hear your music, and see you as a performer and not just a writer or singer."[67] The upbeat, rock-based sound of *Breakaway* proved to be perfect for a concert setting. "I want my music to have just a lot of life—to where people want to get up and jump around," Clarkson declared. "That's the concert I want to have. People let loose and don't care what's going on. They're not worried about work, they're not worried if they've had a bad time with their girlfriend or wife or husband. They're just having fun."[68]

No Time for Love

Between recording, touring, and making public appearances, Kelly Clarkson has very little time for romance. Even though many of her lyrics talk about relationships and heartbreak, the singer admitted in a 2007 interview that she had only had a few boyfriends and had never been in love. "I am very old-school, conservative in my thinking when it comes to relationships," she explained. "Love is something you work at. It doesn't come easily. There are going to be bad days. You are going to have to work at loving someone when they're being an idiot. People think they're just going to meet the perfect guy. Don't be ridiculous."

Clarkson claimed that her realistic view of relationships made it difficult for her to imagine ever getting married. "I'm not really keen on marriage," she acknowledged. "I don't let many people in. Men come and go. Friends are what I care about." If a man does manage to turn Clarkson's head, he is unlikely to be a classically handsome model or actor. "I can't stand pretty boys," she declared. "The guys I date are the just-rolled-out-of-bed, scruffy type. Baseball cap, flannel shirt."

Allison Glock, "Rebel Yell," *Elle*, July 2007, p. 156.

Clarkson won Grammy Awards for Best Pop Vocal Album and Best Female Pop Vocal Performance in 2006.

Winning Awards

The success of *Breakaway* not only translated into hit songs and a popular concert tour, but it also helped establish Clarkson as one of the leading artists in the American music industry. Her work received a great deal of recognition, including a

2005 People's Choice Award for Best Female Recording Artist, and back to-back MTV Video Music Awards for Best Female Video (for "Since U Been Gone" in 2005 and "Because of You" in 2006).

Clarkson also won two prestigious Grammy Awards in 2006. *Breakaway* was honored as the Best Pop Vocal Album of the year, while "Since U Been Gone" was recognized as the Best Female Pop Vocal Performance. When she received her awards, Clarkson gave two lengthy, tearful acceptance speeches. Although she thanked her friends and family, as well as many other people who had contributed to her success, Clarkson did not mention *American Idol*. When reporters asked her about this later, she explained that,

> I didn't expect to win. I didn't know what to say. I'd talk, and I'd cry… But I love where I came from. [*Idol*] is a great idea. For an unknown to come into the business is really hard. I wasn't the ideal picture-perfect pop-star look-alike. It's a cool way for real talent, for people who want it and have the drive, to go the extra mile.[69]

Even though Clarkson did not go out of her way to acknowledge *American Idol's* role in her career, Fuller claimed that he felt no resentment toward the singer. "I'm extremely proud that Kelly won two Grammys for this album," he stated. "No one deserves it more than her. As our first winner, Kelly will always be a big part of the *American Idol* legacy."[70]

Chapter 5

Miss Independent

Despite the success of *Breakaway*, Kelly Clarkson faced an ongoing struggle to take full creative control over her work. She felt that the next obvious step in her artistic development was to write all the songs for her third album, *My December*. However, Clive Davis, the head of RCA Records, was opposed to this idea. Their disagreement over the album's content was publicized by the media in the spring of 2007, leading to some uncertainty about Clarkson's future.

Staying Down-to-Earth

Clarkson's two Grammy Awards for 2005's *Breakaway* confirmed her status as one of the best artists on the American music scene. Clarkson's popularity continued in 2006, even though she released only one new single, "Walk Away." Clarkson was the most-played artist on American radio for the year, and had at least one song ranked in the *Billboard* Top 40 for a record 111 weeks.

Many other young singers and musicians who have reached similar levels of fame have struggled with their new celebrity status. The popular music industry is well-known for producing self-centered and spoiled stars. Clarkson, however, stayed remarkably down-to-earth. Instead of turning into a demanding diva, she remained friendly, outgoing, and accessible. Simon Fuller argued that Clarkson's personality played an important role in her appeal to fans. "I can't think of anyone who sings better than Kelly Clarkson," he said. "She is the best young singer

Maintaining a Positive Body Image

Since she first came to public attention on *American Idol*, Kelly Clarkson has often been mentioned as a positive influence on young women because she projects a healthy body image. Unlike many popular actresses and models—whose rail-thin appearance sets a standard that is unrealistic for most people—the singer is a normal size and proud of it.

At one time, however, Clarkson struggled with issues of weight and self-acceptance. As a freshman in high school, she lost a part in a musical to a less talented girl who was thinner and more attractive than Clarkson. At that impressionable age, Clarkson concluded that she had to lose weight if she hoped to be successful. "The lesson I took from that was purely superficial," she recalled. "It wasn't smart. I headed straight into an eating disorder and became bulimic for the next six months." Fortunately for Clarkson, a male friend found out about her destructive pattern of binge eating and vomiting. She felt so ashamed that she immediately stopped the risky behavior.

Since becoming a star, Clarkson has managed to maintain a positive attitude about her size. "I'm definitely thicker than most people in the industry, but not in real life. When you're on the red carpet with people who weigh 100 pounds, hell yeah I'm bigger than most of them," she acknowledged. "I think it's good for people to see normal. I love food far too much."

"Kelly Clarkson's Bulimic Past," *ET Online*, June 22, 2007. Available online at http://www.etonline.com/celebrities/spotlight/48684.

in the world right now. She is a global superstar. And fans really identify with her, because of her openness. You feel like she is a friend, that you know her. That sets her apart."[71]

Even though Clarkson had gained fame and fortune, she seemed determined to live her life the same way she did before *American Idol*. She hung out with the same group of friends,

Despite winning prestigious awards, Clarkson stayed remarkably down-to-earth and grateful for her success.

Promoting NASCAR

Kelly Clarkson's positive image has led to a number of marketing opportunities. She posed with a milk mustache, for instance, as part of the "Got Milk?" advertising campaign. In early 2007, Clarkson signed a deal to promote NASCAR, the professional stock-car racing league. Her involvement included performing in concert at the Daytona 500, appearing in television commercials, and working as an ambassador for NASCAR charities. "Anyone who knows me knows I'm a race fan and love NASCAR," Clarkson stated. "It's been cool doing things with NASCAR in the past and I'm honored to have the opportunity to play such a huge role in the sport in 2007."

"Kelly Clarkson, NASCAR Ink Deal," *UPI News Track*, January 18, 2007.

enjoyed the same pastimes, and wore the same casual clothing. In fact, Clarkson did not seem to mind being photographed with messy hair and no makeup. "Everyone tells me that the time has come for me to act like a diva. But to be honest with you, I never brush or blow-dry my hair unless I've got to be somewhere in public," she admitted. "I'm worried that if I try to become something I'm not, then I know everything else is going to get screwed up."[72]

Instead of getting caught up in the trappings of fame, Clarkson kept her focus on the music itself. "I couldn't give a crap about being a star," she stated. "I've always just wanted to sing and write."[73] Unlike many other pop stars, Clarkson also largely succeeded in keeping her private life out of the tabloids. She never partied at nightclubs, for example, and she avoided dating anyone famous. All in all, Clarkson behaved like a normal person rather than a pampered celebrity. "She appears free of ego or crippling insecurity. She is a normal dress size. She smiles," noted one interviewer. "She is, no caveats, a pop star you can feel good about liking."[74]

Fighting for Control

The graceful manner in which Clarkson handled her fame made her popular with fans as well as many people within the recording industry. As it turned out, Clarkson needed all of that support and goodwill when she became involved in a high-profile battle with her record company.

The troubles began when Clarkson went to work on her third album, *My December*, in 2006. She hoped to build upon the success of *Breakaway* by creating an album that was even more representative of her musical style and interests. For Clarkson, this meant writing all the songs that would appear on the album. "Clarkson wanted her next album to be more personal, to reflect her experiences and sensibilities, and she decided not to work with the professional songwriters and producers who had previously supplied her with infectious anthems,"[75] one reviewer explained.

When *Breakaway* producer Clive Davis learned of Clarkson's plans, however, he expressed doubts about putting out an album made up entirely of her own songs. "Kelly has shown writing ability, and I think she's probably going to want to try her hand at writing all her material in the future," he acknowledged. "I don't want to dismiss it, I'm rooting for her, but we'll see."[76]

Clarkson expected to face some doubts from Davis and other RCA executives. After all, *Breakaway* had earned so much money for the label that she felt certain they would want to follow the same formula in the hope of repeating its success. But Clarkson also believed that the enormous sales of her previous album put her in a strong position to try something new and to express herself artistically. "My resistance upsets a lot of people, because we could make a lot of money. And I'm not hatin' on money," she explained. "I'm just not comfortable doing things that don't feel like me."[77]

In the end, Clarkson decided to follow her instincts and put together the kind of album she wanted. "There's always this battle, and it's not a bad battle to have. I mean, you obviously don't want 'yes' people around you. And [Davis] and others at the label have been in the business far longer than I have.

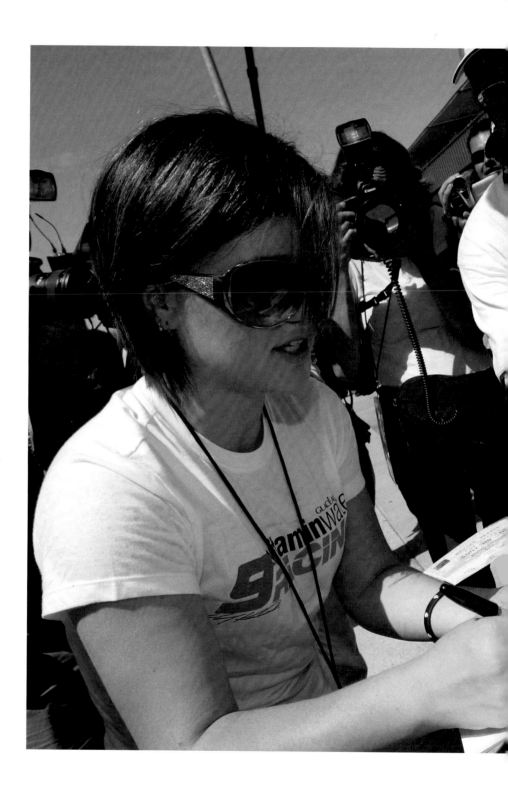

The graceful manner in which Clarkson handled fame made her popular with fans. Their support helped her through a difficult time with her record company.

So obviously you take their opinions in," she noted. "Ultimately, though, I always go with my gut. My gut has done pretty well for me, so I don't see why I shouldn't keep listening to it."[78]

Taking Creative Risks

Clarkson's gut told her to write a collection of songs that explored some of her experiences and emotions since the release of *Breakaway*. "So much has happened," she noted. "*My December* is the story of me over the last couple of years, going through great times, bad times, and bitter times. My life has just been a roller-coaster. I'm finally getting all that out there."[79]

As *My December* began to come together, it became clear that most of the songs Clarkson wrote had a darker, angrier feel than her previous work. Her lyrics were more complicated than before, and her melodies moved further away from pop and toward an edgier rock sound. Although Clarkson realized that these changes might make the new album less popular than *Breakaway*, she was willing to take that risk in order to express herself as an artist. "Some of the songs are not what 10-year-olds are probably going to listen to," she acknowledged. "This record is more intense, it's more raw, it's more emotional... Even if it does tank, who cares? It's one album! Out of a whole career of albums I'm going to have."[80]

Although Clarkson claimed that she did not care whether *My December* sold well, Clive Davis wanted to release an album that would be commercially successful. When the RCA Records chief heard the songs that Clarkson had selected for the album, he became very upset. He complained that the album was too negative in tone and lacked an obvious, radio-friendly hit. In fact, Davis was so concerned about the tone of the album that he reportedly offered Clarkson $10 million to drop five of her original songs and replace them with others of his choosing. Clarkson, however, insisted that she was happy with the album and refused to make significant changes to it. "If I were to make *Breakaway II*, I would have failed myself," she explained. "I don't mind sucking, as long as it is my decision."[81]

Facing Controversy

Arguments over the content of *My December* delayed the release of the album for several months. During that time, both Davis and Clarkson discussed the situation publicly and spoke to the

The release of Clarkson's album My December was delayed due to problems with her record company. She discussed the situation publicly and stood by her decisions while promoting the album.

media about their views. The singer argued that her past successes should allow her to make her own decisions about the future direction of her career. She claimed that sexist attitudes prevented recording executives from taking her seriously. "I've sold more than 15 million records worldwide, and still nobody listens to what I have to say," she stated. "Because I'm 25 and I'm a woman."[82]

Clarkson also expressed frustration that RCA did not want to release an album that contained all her own songs. "I'm a good singer, so I can't possibly be a good writer. Women can't possibly be good at two things," she said of the record label's attitude. "I haven't lost my temper about it. It only drives me more. If your thing is to bring me down, cool. I'll just work harder."[83]

Clarkson's refusal to give up her fight was supported by the media. A number of sources approved of Clarkson's wish to develop as an artist, rather than just sell records and make money. "Give Clarkson the props for fighting for a record she's proud of," one writer declared. "It's refreshing to see a young woman, both successful and with this kind of appeal, exercising this much determination."[84]

Others said that Clarkson's view, though understandable, was simply not realistic in the fiercely competitive music business. "Good for Clarkson for sticking to her guns, for staying true to herself, for answering the muse," noted one writer.

> But the depressing fact is that in today's music climate, one dud of an album can derail a career, especially that of a Top 40 queen. Clarkson is talented, but she's also relatively new. Her fan base is young and fickle. And it's hard to blame Davis for wanting—needing—one of the precious few artists who still sells albums to stay solvent.[85]

Mounting Troubles

Davis's view seemed to ring true when in April 2007, RCA released the first single from *My December*. "Never Again"—an angry, pounding rock song about a bad breakup with

In spite of mounting troubles with her label, Kelly's strong fan base and powerful singing skills resulted in continued marketing opportunities, including performing in 2007 as part of the National Football League's opening kickoff concert with Faith Hill and John Mellencamp.

a boyfriend—initially made it into the *Billboard* Top 10. It received limited radio airplay, however, and dropped quickly down the charts.

Shortly after the release of the single, Clarkson appeared on *American Idol Gives Back*, a special episode of the show that was intended to raise money for charity. Her record label tried to convince her to sing "Never Again" on the program, but Clarkson refused. She felt that it was inappropriate for her to use the TV appearance as an excuse to push her new album. "To promote yourself on a charity event is beyond crass," she stated. "People are starving and dying and I'm up there singing some bitter pop song? And believe me, everyone wanted me to sing it. Because they are jaded and they have no soul."[86]

Instead, Clarkson chose to sing an inspirational folk song, written by Patty Griffin, called "Up to the Mountain." She invited British guitar legend Jeff Beck to accompany her, and their moving performance brought many people in the audience to tears. "She was incredible," Simon Cowell declared afterward. "When you let her come back on the show it makes everybody else look like an amateur."[87]

American Idol featured in the dispute between Clarkson and RCA again a few weeks later. During one of the final episodes of the show's sixth season, Davis appeared on the air to provide viewers with an update on the recording careers of previous winners. While he showered praise on several former contestants— such as 2005 winner Carrie Underwood, who had enjoyed considerable success as a country singer—Davis did not mention Clarkson or her upcoming album. Many analysts noticed the omission and wondered if it meant that there were serious problems with the quality of *My December*.

These rumors received increased media attention in early June, when Clarkson fired her manager, Jeff Kwatinetz of The Firm. She claimed that she had made the difficult decision to let Kwatinetz go because he had not provided her with enough support during her battle with RCA. The singer appeared to be in even greater turmoil a few days later, when she announced her decision to cancel the thirty-one-city U.S. concert tour that had been scheduled to promote *My December*. Clarkson explained that ticket sales for the shows had been lower than expected, partly due to the controversy surrounding her album. "In the craziness of the music business, performing is what I look forward to doing the most, so it is really disappointing to me to have to tell you that I won't be coming out to tour this summer," she said on her website. "But I promise you that we're going to get back out there as soon as humanly possible to give you a show that is even better."[88]

Receiving Mixed Reviews

By the time *My December* was finally released on June 26, 2007, the album had been at the center of a storm of controversy for several months. "The buildup has been nothing short of astonishing," noted one reviewer, "as the blogs, newspapers, magazines, and TV shows have pounced on every fresh development."[89]

When they actually listened to Clarkson's work, however, a number of critics had to admit that the whole situation had been blown out of proportion. They generally agreed that *My December* was not terrible, as the media coverage had led many people to expect, but also not of the same consistently high quality as *Breakaway*. "The original American Idol is fighting a good fight, one that will likely help her career in the long run," wrote one critic. "Unfortunately, *My December* isn't as good as her intentions. Not only will it not match the popularity of *Breakaway*, which featured a string of hits, but it's not as artistically sure-footed."[90]

Several reviewers spoke about the way that Clarkson focused on darker emotional themes in the material she wrote for *My December*. "There are striking personal elements to many of these songs," one critic argued. "She's sad, she's angry, she's exhausted, and the catharsis of singing about her emotions in her own words often lends an extra note of passion to her vocals."[91] While critics appreciated the personal lyrics of many of Clarkson's songs, they felt uncomfortable with her raw expressions of anger and bitterness in others. "*My December* offers an appealing if uneven snapshot of a girl with a big voice and big emotions who's in transition, looking to express herself," stated one reviewer. "The inaugural *American Idol* champ's rage and despair make for an album that can feel unremittingly bleak at times and righteously rocking at others."[92]

On the whole, critics felt that most of the songs on *My December* did not make maximum use of Clarkson's vocal talents. A *Washington Post* reviewer, for example, wrote that "Clarkson sounds shrill throughout *My December*, which is surprising, given just how gorgeous her voice can be."[93] Similarly, a critic for *The Guardian* accused Clarkson of using "her opulent voice as a battering ram"[94] on many of the album's tracks.

The critics made an exception for the last song on the album, "Irvine," which showcased Clarkson's voice alongside an acoustic guitar. A *Newsday* reviewer called the song "achingly beautiful" and said it provided "an example of what Clarkson is capable of and her rare talent to be innovative and incredibly likable at the same time."[95] Describing "Irvine" as "a timeless song of deep longing," a *Hartford Courant* critic wrote that Clarkson "sings sweetly in a low, dusky tone that is heart-stopping. It's a far cry from the manufactured pop of, say, 'Miss Independent,' and it's the unmistakable sound of an artist pushing herself to grow."[96]

Earning New Respect

Although the content of *My December* received mixed reviews, Clarkson's determination to make an album on her own terms earned her the respect of many critics. Several analysts pointed out that it was unfair to judge the value of the singer's work just by the level of commercial success it achieved. After all, some of the best music often only appeals to a small group of people. In addition, unsuccessful albums have been an important step in the career development of many great musicians. "For an artist to grow over a creative lifetime," explained a critic for the *Los Angeles Times*, "she needs to take side roads and make mistakes."[97]

Even though the results of her efforts on *My December* were uneven, many people felt that Clarkson deserved praise for developing her artistic style. "Kelly Clarkson is much too talented to make an awful record. So when she veers off course … it's forgivable and even encouraged—if only as a swift learning lesson in her blossoming career," one reviewer stated. "With *My December*, Kelly Clarkson has proven she has the courage and the diversity to helm what is undoubtedly going to be a golden career."[98]

Although the controversy that swirled around *My December* was unfortunate in many ways, some music industry insiders believed that the struggle could benefit Clarkson in the long run.

Clarkson's determination to make an album on her own terms earned her the respect of many critics. In 2007, she won Song of the Year honors at the ASCAP Awards.

By standing up to those who doubted her, the singer showed courage and integrity. She moved far beyond her beginnings as a reality-show winner to develop as a mature, independent artist who seemed worthy of respect. "Kelly Clarkson has proven to be a strong and independent 'good girl' for women to look up to in this industry," said author and self-esteem expert Jessica Weiner. "She was the first big winner of *American Idol* and I think she could have gone in a lot of different directions, but she's really stayed true to herself, and you can see it."[99]

Introduction: Charting Her Own Course

1. Quoted in Howard Cohen, "Miss Independent," *Miami Herald*, June 30, 2006.
2. Quoted in Ed Bark, "Idol Winner Keeps Up Hectic Pace, But Really, She Just Wants to Sing," *Dallas Morning News*, June 9, 2003.
3. Quoted in Allison Glock, "Rebel Yell," *Elle*, July 2007, p. 156.

Chapter 1: A Small-Town Texas Girl

4. Quoted in Jason Lynch, "From Idol to Star?" *People*, April 28, 2003, p. 71.
5. Quoted in Douglas Perry, "American Idle," *Fort Worth Star-Telegram*, March 2, 2003.
6. Quoted in Perry, "American Idle."
7. Quoted in Perry, "American Idle."
8. Quoted in Barry Koltnow, "She Enjoys the Moment: Kelly Clarkson Feasts on the Fruits of Winning *American Idol*," *Orange County Register*, June 18, 2003.
9. Quoted in Skip Hollandsworth, "Since She's Been Gone," *Texas Monthly*, May 2005, p. 150.
10. Quoted in Lynch, "From Idol to Star?"
11. Quoted in Terrina Hussein, "From Country Girl to Pop Star," *Asia Africa Intelligence Wire*, February 19, 2005.
12. Quoted in Josh Tyrangiel "Miss Independent," *Time*, February 13, 2006, p. 68.
13. Quoted in Hussein, "From Country Girl to Pop Star."
14. Quoted in Lynch, "From Idol to Star?"

Chapter 2: Becoming the First American Idol

15. Quoted in Bud Kennedy, "Kelly Clarkson Getting By with a Little Help from Her Friends," *Fort Worth Star-Telegram*, September 27, 2002.

16. Quoted in Kennedy, "Kelly Clarkson Getting By with a Little Help from Her Friends."
17. Simon Cowell, *"I Don't Mean to Be Rude, But...."* New York: Broadway Books, 2003.
18. Quoted in "Kelly Clarkson," *Biography Today*, Vol. 12. Detroit: Omnigraphics, 2003.
19. Quoted in Tom Gliatto, "On with the Showdown!" *People,* September 9, 2002, p. 52.
20. Quoted in Mark Brown, "Just *Thankful:* Clarkson Happy She Did Things Her Way on TV Show, CD," *Rocky Mountain News,* April 12, 2004, p. D8.
21. Andrew Marton, *"American Idol* Winner Has Warmth and Charm to Spare," *Fort Worth Star-Telegram,* September 4, 2002.
22. Quoted in "Kelly Clarkson," *Biography Today.*
23. Quoted in Lynch, "From Idol to Star?"
24. Brill Bundy, "Live on Tape: In the Audience for *American Idol,"* *Zap2It.com* (via Knight-Ridder/Tribune News Service), August 14, 2002.
25. Quoted in Marton, *"American Idol* Winner Has Warmth and Charm to Spare."
26. Cowell, *"I Don't Mean to Be Rude, But...."*
27. Quoted in "Kelly Clarkson," *Biography Today.*
28. Bundy, "Live on Tape: In the Audience for *American Idol."*
29. Quoted in Mark Washburn, "Kelly Clarkson Crowned American Idol," *Charlotte Observer,* September 4, 2002.
30. Quoted in Hollandsworth, "Since She's Been Gone."
31. Quoted in "Kelly Clarkson," *Biography Today.*

Chapter 3: Getting Caught in the Whirlwind

32. Quoted in Lynette Holloway, "Act Two," *New York Times,* October 14, 2002, p. C9.
33. Jeff Leeds, "Idol Winners Try Stretching Out Their Fame," *New York Times,* November 3, 2004, p. E1.
34. Quoted in "Kelly Clarkson," *Biography Today.*
35. Quoted in Perry, "American Idle."
36. Quoted in Brown, "Just Thankful."

37. Quoted in Perry, "American Idle."
38. Quoted in Hollandsworth, "Since She's Been Gone."
39. Quoted in Perry, "American Idle."
40. Quoted in "Kelly Clarkson," *Biography Today*.
41. Quoted in Brown, "Just Thankful."
42. Quoted in Perry, "American Idle."
43. Quoted in Ron Martinez, "Clarkson Having a Fair Old Time," *Milwaukee Journal-Sentinel*, August 6, 2003.
44. Quoted in Jon Bream, "Beyond 15 Minutes," *Minneapolis Star-Tribune*, June 15, 2003.
45. Quoted in "Kelly Clarkson Crowd-Surfing Diva," MTV.com, February 17, 2004. Available online at http://www.mtv.com.
46. Quoted in Tyrangiel, "Miss Independent."
47. Henry Goldblatt, "Win Beneath Her Wings," *Entertainment Weekly*, April 25, 2003, p. 149.
48. Joanna Hensley, *Lafayette Journal and Courier*, May 9, 2003.
49. Quoted in Tyrangiel, "Miss Independent."
50. Stephen Holden, "Cotton Candy Effigies and a Best Friend from Hell," *New York Times*, June 21, 2003, p. B13.
51. Quoted in Bream, "Beyond 15 Minutes."
52. Quoted in R.D. Heldenfels, "American Idol Star Is Anything but Idle," *Akron Beacon Journal*, July 31, 2003.

Chapter 4: Breaking Away

53. Quoted in Don Thrasher, "What Could Have Been a Reality-Show Novelty, Kelly Clarkson Turned into a Real Pop-Music Career," *Dayton Daily News*, August 14, 2005, p. F1.
54. Quoted in Allison Glock, "Rebel Yell," *Elle*, July 2007, p. 156.
55. Quoted in S. Tia Brown, "Success Stories," *Teen People*, March 1, 2006, p. 64.
56. Quoted in Gary Graff, "No False Idol," *Cleveland Plain Dealer*, April 8, 2005, p. 4.
57. Quoted in Graff, "No False Idol."
58. Quoted in Graff, "No False Idol."
59. Quoted in Tyrangiel, "Miss Independent."

60. Natalie Nichols, *Los Angeles Times*, December 15, 2004.

61. Review of *Breakaway* for *E Online*, February 17, 2004. Available online at http://www.eonline.com.

62. Chuck Taylor, "Kelly Clarkson: Since U Been Gone," *Billboard*, November 20, 2004, p. 67.

63. Quoted in "Breakaway Bio," *KellyClarkson.com*. Available online at http://www.kellyclarkson.com.

64. Chuck Taylor, "Kelly Clarkson: Behind These Hazel Eyes," *Billboard*, April 9, 2005, p. 35.

65. Quoted in "Breakaway Bio," *KellyClarkson.com*.

66. Paul Gargano, "Kelly Clarkson," *Hollywood Reporter*, August 3, 2006, p. 2.

67. Quoted in Thrasher, "What Could Have Been a Reality-Show Novelty, Kelly Clarkson Turned into a Real Pop-Music Career."

68. David Burke, "Pop Goes the Idol," *Wisconsin State Journal*, August 6, 2003, p. D1.

69. Quoted in Howard Cohen, "Miss Independent," *Miami Herald*, June 30, 2006.

70. Quoted in "Idol Not Her Idol?" *Cincinnati Post*, February 10, 2006, p. C10.

Chapter 5: Miss Independent

71. Quoted in Glock, "Rebel Yell."

72. Quoted in Hollandsworth, "Since She's Been Gone."

73. Quoted in Glock, "Rebel Yell."

74. Glock, "Rebel Yell."

75. Joan Anderman, "Her Independent Step Went a Little Too Far," *Boston Globe*, June 19, 2007.

76. Quoted in Tyrangiel, "Miss Independent."

77. Quoted in Glock, "Rebel Yell."

78. Quoted in "Kelly Clarkson Nixes Tour over Slow Ticket Sales," CNN.com, June 15, 2007.

79. Quoted in "Kelly Clarkson's Bulimic Past," *ET Online*, June 22, 2007. Available online at http://www.etonline.com/celebrities/spotlight/48684.

80. Quoted in Anderman, "Her Independent Step Went a Little Too Far."

81. Quoted in Glock, "Rebel Yell."

82. Quoted in Glock, "Rebel Yell."

83. Quoted in Glock, "Rebel Yell."

84. Crystal Olvera, "Music Industry Filled with Sellouts," *Valley Morning Star*, June 18, 2007. Available online at http://www.thev247.com.

85. Anderman, "Her Independent Step Went a Little Too Far."

86. Quoted in Glock, "Rebel Yell."

87. Quoted in Glock, "Rebel Yell."

88. Quoted in "Kelly Clarkson Nixes Tour over Slow Ticket Sales."

89. Preston Jones, "Kelly Clarkson's Third Album Is Littered with Seething Heartbreak," *Fort Worth Star-Telegram*, June 26, 2007.

90. Glenn Gamboa, "Kelly Clarkson's New CD *My December*," *Newsday*, June 26, 2007.

91. Eric R. Danton, "*My December* by Kelly Clarkson," *Hartford Courant*, June 26, 2007.

92. Sarah Rodman, "Ex-Idol Shares Grief and Grit," *Boston Globe*, June 25, 2007.

93. J. Freedom du Lac, "Kelly Clarkson, Striking Out on Her Own," *Washington Post*, June 26, 2007, p. C1.

94. Caroline Sullivan, "Kelly Clarkson: *My December*," *The Guardian*, June 22, 2007.

95. Gamboa, "Kelly Clarkson's New CD *My December*."

96. Danton, "*My December* by Kelly Clarkson."

97. Ann Powers, "Kelly Clarkson's Dispute with Clive Davis Has Made Her Music Hard to Hear," *Los Angeles Times*, June 26, 2007.

98. Brendan Butler, "Kelly Clarkson's *My December*," CB Music, June 25, 2007. Available online at http://www.cinemablend.com/music.

99. Quoted in "Lessons for Bad Girls," Showbiz Tonight, CNN, June 12, 2007.

1982

Kelly Brianne Clarkson is born on April 24 in Fort Worth, Texas.

1988

Clarkson's parents divorce, dividing her family and forcing her to become more self-reliant.

1995

A junior-high music teacher hears Clarkson singing in the hallway and invites the seventh-grader to join the school choir. After her solo at a school assembly receives a standing ovation, Clarkson sets her sights on becoming a professional singer.

2001

Clarkson moves to Los Angeles in hopes of breaking into the music industry, but she is forced to return home to Texas four months later when her apartment is destroyed by fire.

2002

At the urging of a friend, Clarkson tries out for the reality-TV singing competition *American Idol*. Her strong voice and engaging personality help her advance to the finals, where she defeats rival Justin Guarini to win a million-dollar recording contract.

2003

After several delays, Clarkson releases her first album, *Thankful*, in April. By the end of the year it sells a respectable two million copies to be certified double platinum by the Recording Industry Association of America. Clarkson also co-stars in a forgettable movie with Justin Guarini, *From Justin to Kelly*, and finishes second in the inaugural *World Idol* singing competition.

2004

Clarkson releases her second album, *Breakaway*, which features several of her own compositions. Its harder-edged, rock-oriented sound distances her from *American Idol* and earns her critical acclaim and two Grammy Awards.

2005

Clarkson is a featured performer during telecasts of the NFL Super Bowl and the NBA All-Star Game. She also appears as a musical guest on *Saturday Night Live*.

2006

Clarkson is the most-played artist on American radio for the year.

2007

Following a highly publicized battle with Clive Davis and RCA Records over her decision to write all of her own material, Clarkson releases her long-awaited third album, *My December*.

For More Information

Books

Biography Today, vol. 12. Detroit: Omnigraphics, 2003. This readable biography covers Clarkson's early life, her victory on *American Idol*, and the release of her first album.

Contemporary Musicians, vol. 53. Farmington Hills, MI: Thomson Gale, 2005. This reference chronicles Clarkson's musical career through the release of her second album, *Breakaway*.

Current Biography, September 2006. New York: Wilson, 2006. This resource provides a detailed look at Clarkson's life and career, concluding with her Grammy Award wins for *Breakaway*.

Periodicals

Allison Glock, "Rebel Yell," *Elle*, July 2007, p. 156. In this lengthy feature, Clarkson gives her perspective on the controversy surrounding her third album, *My December*.

Skip Hollandsworth, "Since She's Been Gone," *Texas Monthly*, May 2005, p. 150. This cover story offers readers a detailed look at Clarkson's pre-*Idol* struggles to break into the music business.

Andrew Marton, "American Idol Winner Has Warmth and Charm to Spare," *Fort Worth Star-Telegram*, September 4, 2002. Published in the wake of her *American Idol* victory, this feature article from Clarkson's hometown newspaper explores the singer's background.

Douglas Perry, "American Idle: Kelly Clarkson Tries to Maintain Momentum," *Fort Worth Star-Telegram*, March 2, 2003. This feature article provides an update on Clarkson's life after *American Idol* and her efforts to release her first album.

Web Sites

American Idol (http://www.americanidol.com). The official Web site for the Fox TV program features highlights of each season, information on contestants, news updates, photos, and other information for fans.

Kelly Clarkson (http://www.kellyclarkson.com). Clarkson's official Web site offers a biography, news updates, tour dates, and links to sources of more information.

Picture Credits

Cover: © Lucy Nicholson/Reuters/Corbis
AP Images, 14, 26, 31, 35, 36, 40, 43, 61, 83, 87
© Chris Pizzello/Reuters/Corbis, 68
20th Century Fox/The Kobal Collection/Farmer, Jon/The Picture Desk, Inc., 54
Getty Images, 9, 25, 28, 39, 49, 62, 67, 71
Getty Images for NASCAR, 79
Time & Life Pictures/Getty Images, 19
© Tom Fox/Dallas Morning News/Corbis, 23
WireImage/Getty Images, 10, 13, 17, 32, 47, 52, 57, 75, 81

Laurie Collier Hillstrom is a partner in Northern Lights Writers Group, a writing and editorial services firm based in Brighton, Michigan. She has written and edited award-winning reference works on a wide range of subjects, including American history, biography, popular culture, and international environmental issues. Recent works include *Frida Kahlo: Mexican Portrait Artist* (Lucent/Thomson Gale, 2007); *The Thanksgiving Book* (Omnigraphics, 2007); *Television in American Society Reference Library* (3 volumes, UXL/Thomson Gale, 2006), and *The Industrial Revolution in America* (9 volumes, ABC-Clio, 2005–07).